"I MAY BE LITTLE"

THE STORY OF DAVID'S GROWTH

By Marilyn Lashbrook

Illustrated by Stephanie McFetridge Britt

ME TOO!
B O O K S

ROPER PRESS, INC.
DALLAS, TEXAS

Preschool children sometimes feel
very small. Older brothers and sisters
and neighbor children are able to do
so many things. Through the story
of David, your little one will learn
that doing little jobs well will lead to
bigger things. Involve your child in
the story each time by allowing him
to count the sheep on pages 12 and
13. Once your little one knows the
story, pause when you come to a
highlighted word and wait for your
child to fill in the word.

Library of Congress Catalog Card Number: 87-60262
ISBN 0-86606-429-X

Art direction and design by
  Chris Schechner Graphic Design

"I MAY BE LITTLE"

THE STORY OF DAVID'S GROWTH

By Marilyn Lashbrook

Illustrated by Stephanie McFetridge Britt

Taken from 1 Samuel 16 and 17

ME TOO!
B O O K S

Long ago in a land far away
lived a little boy named David.

He had seven brothers
who were older ...
and bigger ...
and stronger
than David.

They did not want
a little boy in the way
while they were working.

Sometimes David felt
very small and unimportant.

But one day his father gave him
a job of his very own.
He asked David to be a shepherd.

A shepherd is someone
who watches the sheep.

A shepherd counts his sheep
to make sure they are all with him.

You can learn to count the sheep too!

A shepherd leads his sheep
to food and water.
He puts medicine on their scratches.

A shepherd loves his sheep.

David was glad
to have a job to do.

"I may be little
but God will help me
do big things!"

David took his sheep to the grassy hills.
He watched while the big sheep ate lunch.

He laughed when the little lambs romped
and rolled among the wildflowers.

But sometimes David felt lonely.
There was nobody to play with.

So David made up songs
to remind himself
that God was always near.

David spent many hours
talking to God.

They became best friends.

David knew God could help him
become a good shepherd.
God could help him
protect his sheep from hungry animals.

Often, David practiced throwing rocks
with his sling …
and he learned to hit his target
every time.

Once a growling bear came
and chased the little lambs.
Round and round David whirled his sling ...
then *zing-g-g* went a stone through the air.

Whack-k-k went the stone
on the big bear's snout.
Gr-r-r-r went the bear as he zipped away
through the bramble bushes.

Another day a ferocious lion
spied David's sheep.
He wanted lamburgers for lunch!

With one big bound
the lion pounced on a fluffy lamb
and snatched it away from its mama.

There was no time to use his sling.
David ran as fast as he could.
He knew God would help him
save his sheep.

Before the lion knew what happened,
David grabbed him by the mane
and bopped him on the head.

The fluffy lamb was safe ...
and David was happy.
He had done a good job.

"I may be little,
but with God's help
I can do big things!"

ME TOO!
B O O K S

SOMEONE TO LOVE
THE STORY OF CREATION

TWO BY TWO
THE STORY OF NOAH'S FAITH

"I DON'T WANT TO"
THE STORY OF JONAH

"I MAY BE LITTLE"
THE STORY OF DAVID'S GROWTH

Available at your local bookstore
or from
Roper Press
915 Dragon Street
Dallas, Texas 75207